COMMAS SAY "TAKE A BREAK"

written by **MICHAEL DAHL** illustrated by **CHRIS GARBUTT**

PICTURE WINDOW BOOKS
a capstone imprint

Commas are NEVER in a hurry.

Commas like to take a break.

Commas also tell readers when to take a break.

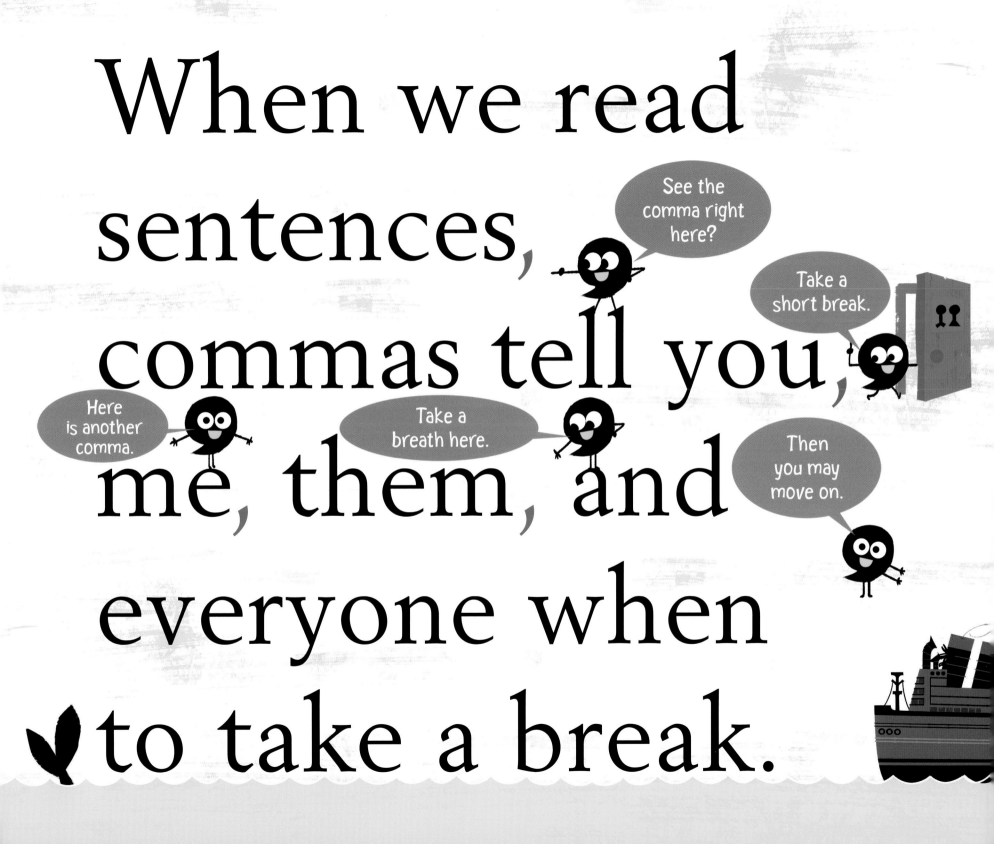

Commas help introduce sentences.

In the swirling sea, the graceful whale was singing.

La, la, la, la, la!

It's very long, but you don't have to worry.

La, la, la, la, la, la, la, la, la, la, la!

The giant, graceful, gray whale was singing in the salty, seaweedy, swirling sea.

The commas help you swim along smoothly.

Commas can take two sentences . . .

The happy whale swam through the sea.

La, la, la, sea-weeeedy!

The jellyfish
floated and
twirled nearby.

. . . and join them together into one long sentence.

Look at the two sentences joined together!

The happy whale swam through the sea, and the jellyfish floated and twirled nearby.

La, la, la! Hello, jellyfish!

Commas also help us write a letter.

A comma
follows a letter's
GREETING . . .

. . . and its
CLOSING.

Dear Whale,
    We hope you have fun
on your trip. Come back
soon! We miss you.

Your friends,
The Gulls
and the Jellys

Commas are very helpful at breaking up long numbers.

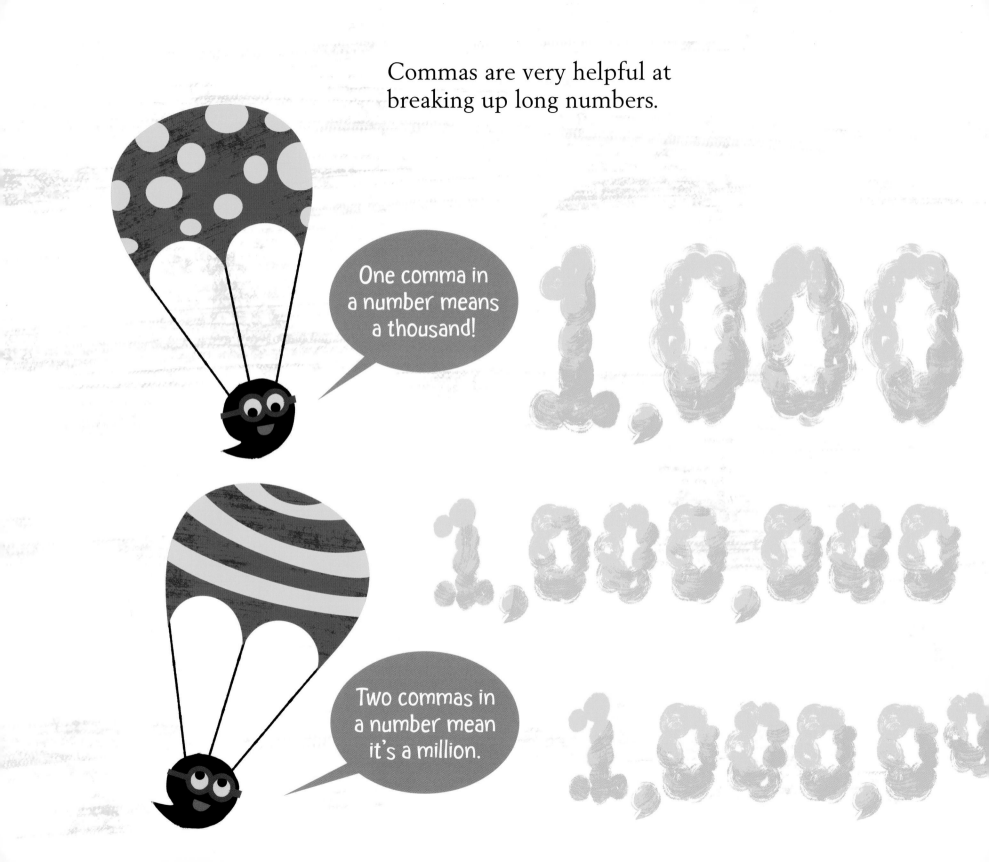

One comma in a number means a thousand!

1,000

Two commas in a number mean it's a million.

1,000,000

1,000,00

Commas are used to SEPARATE A SERIES OF SINGLE WORDS.

The giant, gray, graceful whale likes to sing.

La, la, la, sea-weeeedy!

Commas are also used to SEPARATE A SERIES OF WORD GROUPS.

The whale sang her song, greeted the jellyfish, and went on a vacation.

Hello!

A comma works with a coordinating conjunction TO JOIN SENTENCES that go together.

The whale sang in the swirling sea, and the jellyfish joined her.

La, la, la, la, la, la, la, la!

THE COMMA

Commas are used in LARGE NUMBERS.

Walla Walla, Washington
is 1,000 miles away.

A comma FOLLOWS THE GREETING AND CLOSING in a letter.

Dear Ms. Whale,

Your friend,

Commas SEPARATE DAYS FROM YEARS AND CITIES FROM STATES.

September 6, 2019

Walla Walla, Washington

ABOUT THE AUTHOR

Michael Dahl is the author of more than 200 books for children and has won the AEP Distinguished Achievement Award three times for his nonfiction. He is the author of the bestselling *Bedtime for Batman* and *You're A Star, Wonder Woman!* picture books. He has written dozens of books of jokes, riddles, and puns. He likes to play with words. In grade school, he read the dictionary for fun. Really. And his favorite words are adverbs (*really* is an adverb, by the way).

ABOUT THE ILLUSTRATOR

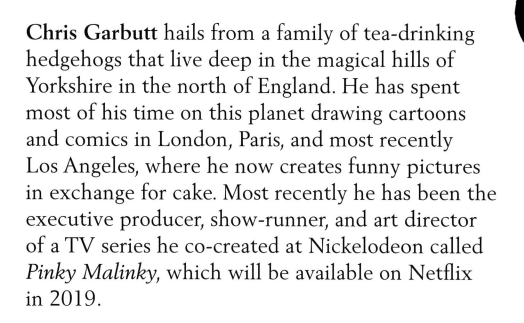

Chris Garbutt hails from a family of tea-drinking hedgehogs that live deep in the magical hills of Yorkshire in the north of England. He has spent most of his time on this planet drawing cartoons and comics in London, Paris, and most recently Los Angeles, where he now creates funny pictures in exchange for cake. Most recently he has been the executive producer, show-runner, and art director of a TV series he co-created at Nickelodeon called *Pinky Malinky*, which will be available on Netflix in 2019.

GLOSSARY

describe—to tell about something

graceful—able to move quickly and easily

greeting—the beginning of a letter

introduction—a part that sets apart the rest of something

seaweedy—full of seaweeds

separate—to set apart

series—a group of related words that come one after another

swirling—moving in a circular motion

Looking for definitions?

READ MORE

Cleary, Brian P. *The Punctuation Station*. Minneapolis: Millbrook Press, Lerner Publishing Group, 2010.

Dahl, Michael. *Periods Say, "Stop!"* Word Adventures. North Mankato, Minn.: Capstone Press, 2019.

Hopkins, Lee Bennett. *A Bunch of Punctuation*. Honesdale, Penn.: Wordsong, 2018.

CRITICAL THINKING QUESTIONS

1. Count the commas on one page of a book. Was it more or less than you expected?

2. Draw a comma, and then draw what it reminds you of.

3. Commas tell us when to take a break. What do you like to do when you take a break?

INTERNET SITES

Use FactHound to find Internet sites related to this book.

Visit *www.facthound.com*

Just type in this code: 9781515838616 and go.

 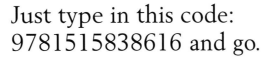 Check out projects, games and lots more at www.capstonekids.com

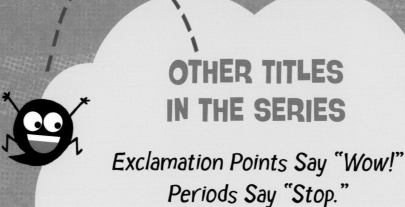

OTHER TITLES IN THE SERIES

Exclamation Points Say "Wow!"
Periods Say "Stop."
Question Marks Say "What?"

Editor: Shelly Lyons
Designers: Aruna Rangarajan and Hilary Wacholz
Creative Director: Nathan Gassman
Production Specialist: Katy LaVigne
The illustrations in this book were created digitally.

Picture Window Books
are published by Capstone,
1710 Roe Crest Drive,
North Mankato, Minnesota 56003
www.mycapstone.com

**Library of Congress Cataloging-in-Publication
Data is available on the Library of Congress
website.**
ISBN 978-1-5158-3861-6 (library hardcover)
ISBN 978-1-5158-4055-8 (paperback)
ISBN 978-1-5158-3865-4 (eBook PDF)

Summary: Commas love taking breaks. In fact, they
want everyone to take breaks! Follow along and
learn all about commas.

Printed and bound in the USA.
PA49